Letters to a Girl

A Perennial Celebration of Growing Up Female

Jennifer Karin Sidford

Letters To A Girl
A Perennial Celebration of Growing Up Female
Created and Edited by Jennifer Karin Sidford

Published by:
Three Sons Publishing
44 Broad Street
Newburyport MA 01950
(800) 838-3544

orders@ThreeSonsPublishing.com
www.LettersToAGirl.org

Copyright © 2005 by Sidford, Jennifer Karin

Publisher's Cataloguing-in-Publication Data
Letters to a girl : a perennial celebration of growing up female/created and edited by Jennifer Karin Sidford. -- Newburport, MA : Three Sons Publishing, 2005.

p. ; cm.

A collection of inspirational letters from 20 women to an imaginary girl, on a variety of life's topics. ISBN: 0-9747095-0-6

1. Girls--Conduct of life. 2. Young women--Conduct of life. 3. Life skills. 4. Women--Correspondence. 5. Letters.
I. Sidford, Jennifer Karin. II. Title.

HQ777 .L48 2004
305.23/082--dc22   0411

PROJECT COORDINATION BY BookMarketingSolutions.com
DESIGN BY CurleyDesign.com

Printed in China

Dedication

For my Granny, Muriel Selden Paris

Mother of three
Grandmother of four
Great-grandmother of eleven
Model of grace and intellect to all

And, I offer my most profound appreciation to the 20 thoughtful women who each donated their time, talent and wisdom toward the creation of this book in support of vital women's housing, health and recreational programs.

Carol Brien	Penny McCabe
Deborah Budden	Natasha Paden
Jane Cosner	Elsie Paris
Jenna Desrochers	Joan Perera
Pam Erickson	Ava Scott
Astrid Galindo	Anna Smulowitz
Betsy Griffith	Kay Stratton
Cricket Hannah	Tarsha White
Sue Hertz	Katie Younes
Kate Knox	Maria Younes

It's in the reach of my arms,
The span of my hips,
The stride of my step,
The curl of my lips.

I'm a woman
Phenomenally.
Phenomenal woman,
That's me.

~ Maya Angelou

Introduction

When you look at the cover of this book, what do you see? Do you wonder what it was like for this little girl to grow up?

Did she face economic hardship and times of prosperity? Liberating moments of society and events to rein it back in? Were there great crimes against humanity that could never have been imagined? Did she, herself, face divorce, a happy marriage, the loss of a child or the blessing of many? Did she see minorities win the right to vote and women challenge the social structure of every household? Did she hear great men speak at the steps of the Capitol and witness courageous boys heading into battle? Did she see men and women fly to the stars and ashes rise from the skyline?

The answer is yes to all these things. This little girl is my grandmother, Mimi Paris. And if you asked her, "do you have the mettle to face all these sorts of issues," she would predictably undersell herself by answering "oh no, I don't think so." But look carefully at this little girl's face. You can see it. The strength, the determination, the intelligence and the spirit; she has everything it takes and then some. We all do.

It is inside all of us from the day we are born. Sometimes, we just need to be reminded of it. Or, more likely, reminded of it constantly — because the day-to-day tedium of life has a way of clouding our view of self.

What every girl needs to flourish in her lifetime is inside her – always has, always will be. And these letters, from 21 seemingly ordinary women, deliver extraordinary messages for every woman and girl that lives today.

Dear girl,

This is for you. Live well.

J.K.S.

Betsy

Elisabeth Griffith, Ph.D., is a mom, historian and Headmistress of The Madeira School. She is the author of In Her Own Right *(Oxford University Press, 1984), a biography of Elizabeth Cady Stanton. Betsy served as a consultant for Ken Burns' PBS documentary about Elizabeth Cady Stanton and Susan B. Anthony. Betsy is also on the advisory board of The White House Project, a non-partisan organization devoted to advancing women into all positions of leadership, including the U.S. presidency.*

My Darling Girl,

Now that you have reached double digits, I've been thinking about what grown-up advice to give a girl growing up. You are already smart, spunky and stouthearted. If I were like those fairy godmothers in Sleeping Beauty, who blessed Aurora at her christening, I would hope that you find two qualities which will strengthen and safeguard you throughout your life.

The first is that you find sources of passion — for people, causes, vocations, honor — for shoes, tennis, teaching, art — whatever you care so strongly about that you will focus your considerable energy on it. My passions have been your grandfather, women's rights, my children, writing, history, and houses. I look forward to watching you discover yours.

The second blessing I would present is perseverance. Perseverance is grittier than passion, but without it you will achieve nothing. I remember when your Aunt Megan and Uncle JD were toddlers learning to walk. Every time they went ker-plop (sometimes sounding soppy if their diapers were wet), we would sing the Broadway ditty, "Pick yourself up, dust yourself off, and start all over again." Perseverance is the "little engine that could," and did, chugging, "I think I can, I think I can."

Like the train, perseverance takes us up mountains, one step at a time, despite blisters or back aches or heavy packs, until we reach the peak. The ability to persevere, to stick to a task until it is completed, to remain committed even when discouraged, to strive for one's goals despite setbacks, requires toughness, stubbornness, guts. You've got all of those.

My favorite story about perseverance is about the fate of the Endurance, the aptly named ship which took British explorers to the South Pole in 1911. Did you see the documentary or museum exhibit about this misadventure? Ernest Shackleton's ship got stuck in the ice. His attention had to shift from success to survival. He managed to outlast the winter, navigate in a small boat through treacherous waters to an inhabited island, take screws from the boat to attach to his boots so he could climb over a mountain range to find help. Not one man perished. Shackleton's courage and endurance are admirable.

There are clearly many examples of equally brave women, many of them too modest or too exhausted to record their daring deeds. But consider Sacajawea, the Shoshone guide and interpreter who led Lewis and Clark across the Louisiana Territory two hundred years ago. Still a teenager and the mother of a two-month-old son with whom she made the journey, Sacajawea was a valued member of the expedition. (One of the reasons I love history is that it prompts me to imagine living these lives.)

Shackleton and Sacajawea persevered in the face of hardships. I hope you never face such life-threatening challenges, but growing up female in America can also be risky. In the way you tackle your homework or practice batting or behave ethically, you are practicing perseverance.

All you can do is "keep on keeping on" or in the words of a favorite school motto, "Function in disaster, finish in style."

Big hugs and cheers,
Betsy

Elsie

In 1945, Elsie Paris worked as a translator of French for the U.S. Government in Europe. She was lucky enough to be one of very few American civilian women to celebrate the end of World War II in Paris, France, where she later met and married her husband and where the first of their five children was born. At age 40 she attended the Harvard Graduate School of Education. Always interested in issues of war and peace, she was active, along with her husband, in studying and promoting non-violent ways of resolving conflict through the national organization, Beyond War, now the Foundation for Global Community. At present she is a devoted grandmother of four, loves gardening and bird watching, and is living in Vermont.

My dear Granddaughter,

You know that today is my 80th birthday! Since you love getting letters, as promised I'm writing a birthday message – just to you – about something wonderful that happened to me in my first eighty years.

I've been trying to think of one special moment or one important event that was the best. But the more I thought about it, the more I realized it was not something that happened just once; it was something that lasted a very, very long time.

What happened was that I had the same best friend for fifty-five years – which is three quarters of my life on this planet. When your grandfather and I fell in love it was very romantic. We met in the beautiful city of Paris near the Eiffel Tower where Madeline lives. He was handsome, kind, loved adventures, and made me laugh. We grew to like each other so much that after only six months – just half a year – we decided to get married. We were always happy being together but, as it happens, in that short time neither of us had ever been sad or angry or sick. So we didn't know much about each other when things were especially hard. We were positive that we'd live happily ever after.

Why were we so sure? Well sometimes when you meet somebody you feel a flash of good magic. It's exciting because the person is new, and it also feels cozy because for some reason the person seems familiar. Grown-ups call this intuition. Children are wonderful at feeling it so you probably know what I mean. But as people grow up, they often forget to trust their intuition – what their eyes and their heart tell them. In our case, what I saw was a man whose eyes twinkled with good humor, who was sweet and smart and witty and kind; what I felt was the strength of a person you could count on to be true-blue in all his relationships with people. The combination was irresistible!

Of course, like all friendships and marriages, ours had its bumpy moments. But love, laced with your grandfather's grace and tenderness and PLENTY of laughter helped to resolve them, even the very difficult ones.

So remember. If you keep your eyes and heart open you'll have the courage to trust your intuition. I bet you'll find the good magic – in a new best friend whose intuition is just like yours, someone who will make you happy, make you laugh, even when you least expect it.

Much, much love,
Your devoted Grandma

Astrid

Astrid Galindo escaped the violence of her country, Colombia, by emigrating to the United States. Upon arrival, she discovered a tumor in her breast. With limited English, Astrid reached out to her local YWCA for health and treatment support. Now fluent in English, Astrid, her husband and their twin sons are thriving. In appreciation for her good health, Astrid became certified as a peer educator in breast self-exams.

Poem

A woman's staff is her kindness,
The intelligence, her imperial crown;
Her best award, a pure soul;
And her reason to exist: true love.

Poema

El cetro de una mujer es su dulzura,
Su corona imperial : La inteligencia;
Su major galardon el alma pura;
y el amor la razon de su existencia.

Acrostic

We are the miracle of creation,
a kind of human whose nature
endowed them with excellent qualities
like intelligence and beauty fair.

Our main goal is to keep our families
and our communities full of love, peace
faith and harmony.

"**M**other, grandmother, aunt, niece and daughter"
those words are meaning a lot, they are synonyms of
"justice, peace, dignity, love and freedom."

Advocates of the just causes, dreamers
of happy worlds, fighters of impossible wars,
hard workers of lovely homes.

Nobody knows more about life than a mother.
Only she can know the
beautiful experience that procreation means.
Only she is able to sacrifice
her own life for her child, only her:
the mother, the woman.

Sue

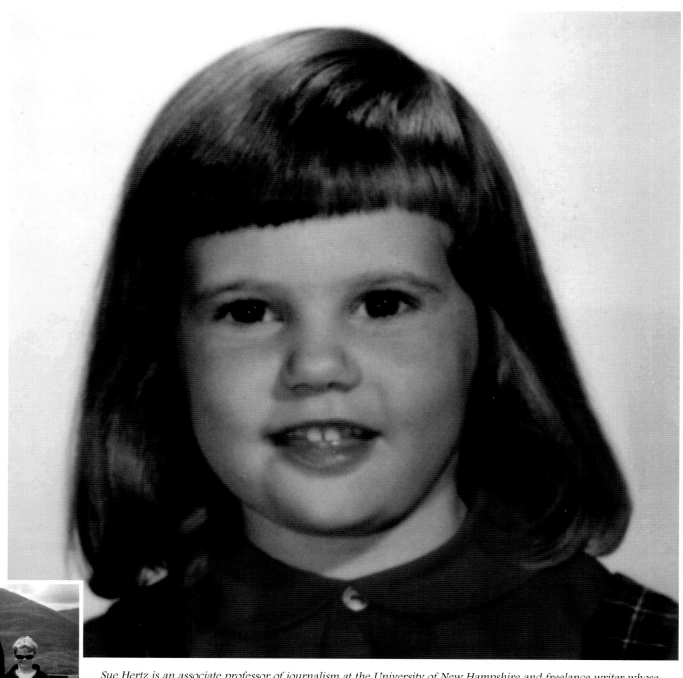

Sue Hertz is an associate professor of journalism at the University of New Hampshire and freelance writer whose work has appeared in national and regional magazines for the past two decades. Author of Caught in the Crossfire: A Year on Abortion's Front Line (Prentice Hall, 1991), Sue is a former newspaper feature writer for The Hartford Courant, The Seattle Post-Intelligencer, and The Herald in Everett, Washington. She lives in Newburyport, Massachusetts, with her husband Bill Steelman and sons Luke and Jordy and yellow lab Riley.

Dear Meg,

      I have always thought that the world is divided into two kinds of people: those who do everything well and easily and those who have to try hard to succeed. I hope that you are lucky enough to be among the latter.

      I once worked with an extraordinarily gifted writer at The Hartford Courant. He'd had his pick of colleges, jobs, writing assignments. Still, he wasn't happy. So unfamiliar with failure was he that when an editor changed a phrase or criticized an idea, he unraveled. Any suggestion that wasn't praise hit him like an assault. He eventually left newspaper work to write fiction. Again, he met success; he published short stories in the most coveted of publications, The New Yorker. Yet he remained melancholy; not all of his submissions were accepted. When so much had come so easily, he retreated at the first obstacle.

      If success doesn't come on the first, second, or even fifth try, you learn how to hurdle rejection. And if you learn how to hurdle rejection, you learn how to have a happy life. Because when you don't make the A soccer team, or get accepted at Vassar, or are second pick for that plum marketing job in Chicago, you'll have two choices: plot out Plan B or wallow in self-pity. Disappointments are inevitable and the cheeriest, most centered, most contented people are those who accept sour news, learn from it, and hatch fresh routes to realize dreams.

      History is packed with people who have overcome defeat, but I don't look further than my own family for proof. At 57, my dad was laid off from a Boston company for which he'd worked for over three decades, and despite heroic efforts could not land a similar position. He weighed his options and decided with my mother to teach in a town on a lake in New Hampshire where they had always wanted to live. Leaving the comfortable Boston suburb and the elegant home with the grand lawn was tough, but he and my mom never looked back. They treasured the mountain views, the evening swims, and the peace of rural life.

      Their flexibility was contagious. Then 16, the only benefit I conceded to the move was that my new high school had an alpine ski team. I had always wanted to race. Yet I didn't make the team. Crushed, I thought of my dad and analyzed my options. I could sit at home after school or try another sport. With the help of a friend, we started the school's first girls' cross-country ski team. We weren't particularly good, but we had a lot of fun, acquired a new skill, and thirty years later, I'm as happy flying through a field of fresh snow on my Nordic skis as I am doing just about anything.

      That lesson has endured. For me, as for everyone, disappointments litter life. Colleges rejected me. Employers rejected me. Editors still reject me. Yet for each "no," I have tried to maneuver around the block to find another avenue to "yes," or at least another route that will make me happy. There is no avoiding what famed psychiatrist Elisabeth Kubler Ross calls "windstorms," life's inevitable losses. You just have to know something better rests elsewhere and persevere to find it.

Only the best to you,
Sue

K a t e

Kate Xin Mei Knox spent the first five and one-half years of her life in China before arriving at her new home in America on November 30, 2001. She completed her first year of formal education with enthusiasm and an insatiable appetite to learn and do more. Entering second grade, she is a highly successful student and a member of her Brownie Troop. She also loves art, dance, swimming and soccer.

Dear Friend,

My name is Kate Xin Mei. I came from China. I have been living in America for one and one-half years. I was afraid when I first saw my new father, mother and brother. I had never seen anyone who was not Chinese. My mother kept telling me not to be afraid. She said I was very brave to come to a new country. I didn't know there would be people who looked like me in America. My mother told me there were many Chinese people living in America. My trip from China to America was a long journey.

When people ask me about China, I tell them 'China was a hard place to live in. America is a fun place! America has many good things for children.' If another girl were coming to America, I would say, 'Don't be afraid. America is a fun place where you will be happy.' I now have both Chinese and American girlfriends in America and a family. I am happy!

Kate Xin Mei

J o a n

Joan Perera grew up in Greenwich, Connecticut in a family with long and deep roots in the town. She graduated from Stanford University and returned to the East Coast to teach. She met her husband during a snowy night when they were both late for a dinner party. "We engaged in conversation during the time-consuming task of removing our boots on the porch. Fourteen months later we were married. Guido and I have three wonderful – and very different – daughters. Each has enriched our lives more than we can say." Currently, you can find Joan giving tours at the Museum of Fine Arts, Boston.

To Polina, my granddaughter, and to any future granddaughters: Thoughts about being Female

As a child in the 1940s and 50s, I didn't think much about being a girl; but at some level, I knew that being a woman stood for something.

As I matured and became an adult, I began to appreciate the strong women who preceded me. Chief among these was my mother, your great grandmother, Grams. Here was a woman who coped. Despite being widowed at age 24 with two small children, Grams carried on and did her best. "You do what you have to do," she often said.

At age 26, she fell in love again and married my stepfather, a man with two children of his own. By the time she was 27, she headed a household of seven, our year-old family of six plus our newborn half-brother. In my young eyes, Grams could do anything.

My mother-in-law was another one of your great-grandmothers. Nana had an eye for clothes, jewelry and the character of people. She was at the center of her family of four sons; and for her, like Grams, home was where the heart was.

So, Polina, based on your name, here are some of my thoughts on living:

Parents - You have started life with a wonderful gift: two parents who love you deeply. Their love is with you and it will be a source of strength your whole life.

Organization - Over the years, I've discovered that life goes more smoothly when I organize and don't "put off" until later those chores I should do right now.

Love - It's important to love yourself. I don't mean pamper yourself, but rather love and nurture your God-given talents. And then you will love others.

Interests - Interests make life richer; and your choices are endless — from music to stamp collecting, tennis to gardening, sewing to rock-climbing — The list is deep and wide.

Nature - Find pleasure in nature. I love the beach with the sound of the waves and the moist salt smell. I look for smooth stones that fit in the palm of my hand. I once found a gray one with a thin white line encircling it. Good luck, I'm told.

Accept yourself as you are - Each one of us is unique, with our own strengths and shortcomings. It takes time to recognize our strengths and honesty to admit our weaknesses. But take the time, the end result — knowing yourself — is worth it.

In closing: Step into life. Do your best. Cherish your female gender!

I love you,
Mimi

Cricket

Lucretia "Cricket" Hanna is a mother of three grown sons. She lives in Warner, New Hampshire where she has ancestral connections that go back seven generations. Cricket has been a Certified Nurse Midwife for 14 years and has birthed approximately 900 babies. She is currently a student in Alberto Villoldo's Healing the Light Body School and has visited Peru twice in the last year to learn from the medicine people the importance of a connection to the earth and to the healing world of Spirit.

Dear Daughter Anna,

     I am writing to you today as this time in your life brings forward changes that will unfold. You can begin to see that who you are should never be underestimated. Your actions affect everything and everyone around you.

     Always remember you are able to make changes to make this world, and all that are part of it, more loving. When you give your love to a friend or to a parent or to a river or to a flower, remember this love returns to you as an unending resource.

     You can never be lonely or unloved as you are connected to all that is.

     You are five years old! You are now becoming every word you say, every smile and every hug you give. Each time you offer these treasures, understand how meaningful each one is to all that is.

     Celebrate with love your beautiful life and honor yourself for what you wish to see yourself become.

     Happy Birthday, Anna! I am glad you were born.

Your Loving Mom

Kay

Kay Stratton (pictured above left with her sister) is the founding chair of MIT's Catherine N. Stratton Lecture Series on aging successfully. She is also actively involved with the MIT Women's League and the MIT Council for the Arts. Kay served several years as a national board member for the YWCA. Kay's husband, Jay Stratton, was president of MIT from 1959-1966. He was also Chairman of the Board of Trustees for the Ford Foundation and served under several US presidents. At the time of this book's publication, their three daughters are planning to take Kay to Italy for her 90th birthday.

Dear Young Girl,

I'm not sure I have a specific message for you other than to always live as full a life as you possibly can and to continue to reach beyond your own and others' expectations.

I've had the most extraordinary life! My early years were difficult. My mother died when I was five, and my father sent my baby sister and me to live with my grandmother and aunt in Virginia. I was not a very nice child. I was always correcting my elders. "Those are not tea cakes, they are cookies", or "those are not drawers, they're panties," I'd say. But somehow I found a way of getting what I needed out of life.

My aunt told me I could not go to college. But full of ambition and determination, I enrolled in summer courses at the University of Virginia, which qualified me for a state teacher's college, now called Mary Washington College — and that step gave me my personal and intellectual freedom.

At 21, I was eager to seek my fortune and was invited to live in Irvington, New York with my best friend and her family. I found a job at a jewelry trade magazine for $14 a week. Of course I had to spend $10 a week to commute into Manhattan, but I was free — a dream come true!

In 1935 my future husband was in New York to give a lecture at Columbia University and asked me for dinner. I had met him 7 years earlier, but I couldn't remember exactly what he looked like. Would I recognize him? When I stepped off the train from Irvington, he was standing in front of me with a warm smile. He said, "Catherine!", and I said, "Jay!" It was love at first sight, which lasted for the 59 wonderful years of our marriage.

We spent much of our life here at MIT and in traveling the world for the Ford Foundation. We had different roles but a very complementary existence. We raised three lovely daughters and were a close family, spending summers on our farm in Vermont.

In his later years, Jay had many health problems. When he was sick, he always wanted me to stay home with him, but I tried very hard to keep on with my outside commitments. I always told him exactly when I would be back. When I returned, he would often say, "You are 10 minutes late!" And I would say, "But you know how hard it is to leave in the final moments of a discussion and I want you to share the ideas, as we've always done together."

But now as older women, we have to work twice as hard against physical disabilities and mental lapses to keep up our involvement in the world around us and to ensure a full and interesting life. If you don't, you just become shadowy.

So plan each day with purpose, have faith in yourself and your dreams, and go for it—because there is always a way!

Kay

Debbie

Debbie Budden is a mother of two young daughters and a teacher of English Literature and Writing.
She has earned degrees from Middlebury College, Oxford University and the University of Massachusetts,
Amherst. She has taught at high schools and colleges in America, England and Austria, and hopes to
continue teaching, and spreading a love of books, for as long as she is able. Deb also loves ice cream.

Dear Sophie, Elizabeth, and all who will journey with you:

When you are young, you already have a certain feeling about books. Someone who is reading to you, or listening to you read, is snuggled up close to you; your hearts are beating next to each other. The book connects you.

Eventually, book-reading will become something you do on your own. You may not have that grown-up snuggling in as you read, but you will continue to have books to keep you company and connect you to others. In fact, as you try to decipher the complex maze that is adolescence, a book can give you a way to explain things you haven't been able to express. You CAN, you WILL find someone in a book who knows how you feel, and, at the same time, teaches you something about yourself.

As you launch out into the big world without your family for the first time as a young adult, a book can make you feel right at home. Like a good talk with your own mother, a book can give you the feeling of shared experience. A book can affirm who you are, and what you have been through, by connecting your life to the words on the page. You say: "That happened to me! I remember when I felt that way! That is what I have been trying to say!" You discover that you are part of a larger world, part of humanity.

As children of the new millennium, you enter into a world that is much different from the world into which I entered. Yours is full of computers, televisions and all sorts of electronic gadgets. I write to you now not to say ignore these gadgets; that would be nearly impossible. Simply remember to let books journey with you through life also. Read, question and consider. It will help you to live and love well. I have learned this through reading, and I pass the message on to you, with much love.

Your mother, teacher, and friend
Debbie

Tarsha

Tarsha White is a graduate of Woman to Woman, a professional development and mentoring program run by Boston's historic Women's Educational and Industrial Union. A single mother to her young daughter Dacia, Tarsha believes parents are a child's first teacher. She works hard everyday to instill a love for learning in Dacia's heart and mind. Tarsha and Dacia also share a love for music, singing and dancing. Tarsha's goal is to become a counselor for battered women.

Woman to Girl

Just take a minute to listen
to some helpful advice.
You may think some of it's corny.
But I'm positive it will make you stop.
And think twice.
Don't be a follower but yet a leader.
Pat yourself on the back.
And be your own cheerleader.
Don't listen to false hype.
Listen to your soul and do what's right.
Stand tall and finish the race.

So what if you lost and came in last place.
You're still a beautiful young lady.
With so much style, poise, and grace.
Fill yourself up with a rich pure soul.
It's a gift that can't be broken,
or stolen
because it's something that you have chosen.
It doesn't take money to be rich.
As long as you have a clean spirit.
It doesn't matter if only you can hear it.
As long as you're willing to pass it on and
share it.

Anna

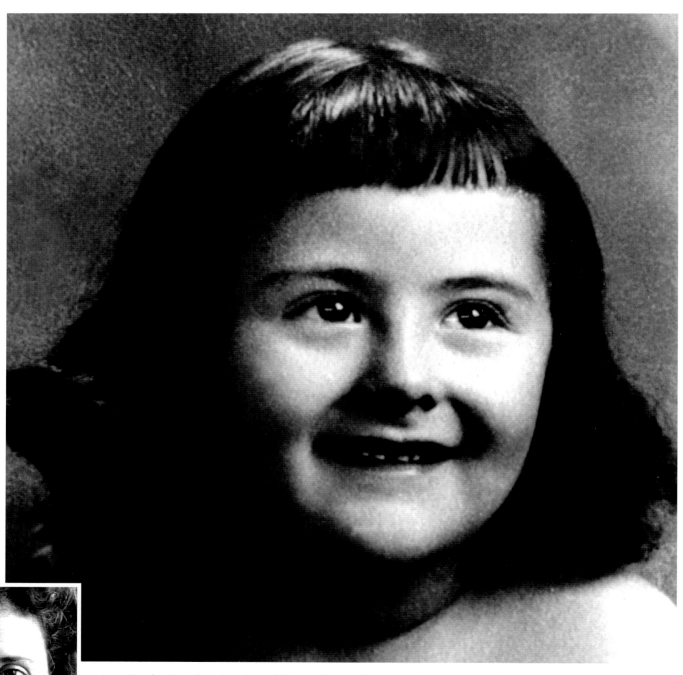

Anna Smulowitz is founder of the children's theatre, Theatre in the Open. Over the years, she has introduced theater to over 3,000 acting students. Currently, she runs a collaboration of actors, directors, designers, writers, choreographers, musicians and stage technicians that provides contemporary and classical theater experiences. Since 1979, Anna has acted in, directed or produced over 100 shows and developed three major summer arts programs. She is an expressive therapist and hospital chaplain at Beverly and Salem Hospitals in Massachusetts. Anna recently appeared on "Dateline NBC" as a daughter of Holocaust survivors.

The Acting Lesson

Director: "OK, when you are feeling inspired, you can begin."

Acting Student: (Hesitates, takes a deep breath and panics.)

Director: "Whenever you're ready. Take your time."

Acting Student: (Wrings her hands together, bites her lip, begins to cry.)
The director patiently waits.

Acting Student: "I can't do this. I'll never be good at this. You're wasting your time with me. I stink."

Director: "I'm not wasting my time as long as you are willing to keep working at it."

Acting Student: "I'll never get it right."

Director: "Do you have a desire to express yourself?"

Acting Student: (trembling) "Yes."

Director: "Then there is no right and wrong. There is only you and your fierce uniqueness. You are on a journey to your highest self. A place where you can let people hear what you have to say, and where you have every right to be heard."

Acting Student: "I'm afraid of being rejected. I feel exposed."

Director: "To be stuck where you are now is to be at the threshold of self-discovery. You can acknowledge your fear and move beyond it or you can decide to turn around and go back. It's like being at the end of a very high diving board. It takes exceptional courage to move beyond your fear but when you do, you take flight and feel the exhilaration of soaring – of accomplishment."

Acting Student: "I'm afraid of breaking my neck."

Director: (Laughs empathetically.) "You can choose to get off the board or you can jump and feel intense joy. It may not be perfect. But you will have tasted accomplishment and you can grow from there."

Acting Student: (Takes another deep breath, smiles and steps forward.)

Carol

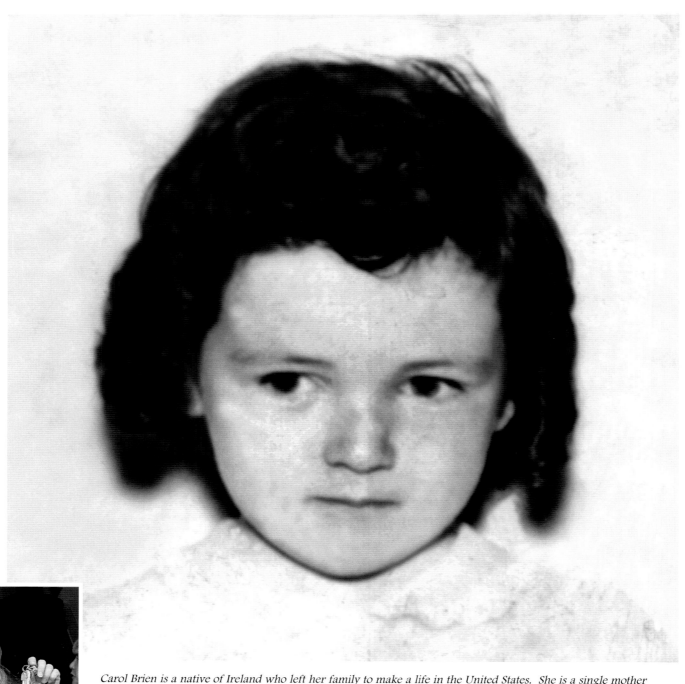

Carol Brien is a native of Ireland who left her family to make a life in the United States. She is a single mother of two children and has overcome an abusive marriage, homelessness and the challenges of returning to college to finish her degree. Carol is pictured holding the keys to her new Habitat for Humanity home she helped earn for her family in April, 2003. In May of the same year, she received a Mother of Inspiration award from The One Family Campaign. A dedicated mother and an eternal optimist, Carol chooses to see the good in people and tries to encourage that whenever possible. She believes deeply in the value and resilience of the female spirit.

Photo: Courtesy of One Family

Dear Tara,

How precious you are! Did I tell you how happy I am that you are a girl? You are filled with all the beauty and wonder of the universe, and you can take pride in knowing that you possess all the qualities to one day make you a strong, capable, compassionate woman. Life seems simple now. Be confident in the knowledge that despite the trials life has in store for you, you have an inner strength and quiet confidence to face your challenges. Be sure to surround yourself with people who are caring and optimistic; they will sustain you through the hard times.

Take pleasure in your family. If you can forgive them for their imperfections and learn by their mistakes, you will be truly blessed. If you find yourself with no family, good friends can bring you just as much joy. You may even want to start a family of your own one day!

I wish for you the love of a partner who will see you for the treasure you are. If you decide to have children, be sure your partner is up for the job. Parenting is a very rewarding but very challenging position. You both will need the training and seriousness required of any other career. Mix this with humor and flexibility, and you will awaken parts of your heart you never knew existed. Know that should destiny or tragedy leave you to face this alone, you have the inner strength to rise to the task.

There are people and resources willing to help you, but you must show them your value and resilience. My children and I were once homeless because of a fire, and were faced with situations I never imagined. But I stayed positive, and refused to accept conditions not suitable for me or my children. I believed in my capabilities and the compassion of others. When faced with adversity, you may find many doors will not open for you. Keep knocking. The right one will eventually open.

If you decide not to have children, that is OK too. You have so much to give to the world and so much to wonder at. Keep your spirit and love of life. Never let anyone decide for you what your beauty is. Dance to your own tune and share your gifts with humanity. Don't settle for situations or relationships that are not respectful or equal to your worth. Believe in yourself. You will have all you need inside of you to do well. You are all you require at any given moment, or for a lifetime. Share your love with the world and take great joy in the fact that you too are lovable.

Love and wishes for now and the future,
Carol

Penny

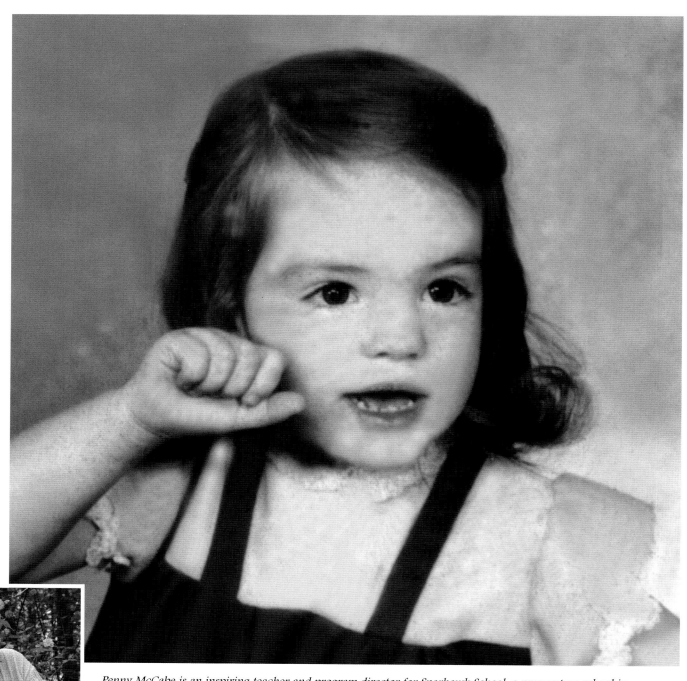

Penny McCabe is an inspiring teacher and program director for Sparhawk School, a preparatory school in Amesbury, Massachusetts. She has the qualities that every parent hopes for in a teacher: the ability to connect with a child and help them blossom with their own talent and determination. Penny was pregnant with her first child when Letters to a Girl was imagined. With perfect connectedness to the book's theme, she delivered a baby girl. Penny quickly adapted her fable to welcome Molly.

Dear Little One,

Late at night as we snuggled together, I began to tell you your first story. It is amazing to think of all that is before you. I already see your curious eyes and those thoughtful expressions and I wonder what you are thinking. What I do know is that you are loved and have an amazing life before you. Remember that as you choose your own path.

With love,
Your Mom Penny

And So The Adventure Begins

One day little Miss Molly Maggee was off on her first adventure into the world. She was thoughtful and curious as she set out. Surrounding her were trees, grass and colors that filled all of the spaces that she could see. As Molly walked along she came upon a tall towering yellow flower. The flower reached out his jagged green arms to greet her.

"Hello, I am Mr. Dandelion." He had vibrant yellow petals for hair and a deep yellow for a face.

"Hello, Mr. Dandelion. What do you do here?" asked Miss Molly.

"Well, Miss Molly, I have a very important job. I have strong, long, deep roots that travel on and on; they hold together the soil for other plants to grow."

Miss Molly looked up with furrowed brows and responded, "Oh fiddlesticks, you can't do all that." And off she went.

As she traveled on she came upon a tall towering oak. It had brilliant shades of greens and browns that stood out against the pale blue sky. She gazed up at the giant beauty and said, "Hello! Who are you and what do you do?"

The tall towering oak leaned down and spoke with a booming voice; "I am Mr. Oak. I have deep roots that travel down into the earth holding it together and leaves that give you the air to breathe."

Miss Molly looked up again with her furrowed brow and said, "Fiddlesticks, you can't do all that." And off she went on her travels.

As she slowly kicked along, she came across a wiggly worm squirming across her path. Again, she said, "Hello!" and asked the worm who he was.

The little worm replied, "I am Mrs. Worm. I have many jobs here. I loosen the soil for all the plants to grow, I give the soil nutrients and, I am sometimes food for the birds that sing throughout the day."

Molly looked down at Mrs. Worm and asked, "How do you do all that?"

Mrs. Worm gazed back and with a thoughtful tone responded, "Miss Molly, I can do anything I want. We all can. Each one of us gets to choose our own path, just as you are doing on your walk. You choose which way to go and what to do along the way."

Molly looked down with a grin and said, "Thank you Mrs. Worm, I do get to choose. Right now, I choose to be a fairy and play in my fort. Goodbye Mrs. Worm."

And as they parted the little wiggly worm called out, "Remember Miss Molly, let your curiosity guide you! You can do anything!"

Jenna

Jenna Desrochers is a recent high-ranking graduate of comparative literature and women's studies from the University of Massachusetts, Amherst. She currently trains and rides Morgan horses and competes in horse shows across New England. She has a great fondness for independent films, darts, fiction and coffee. She has traveled from the rain forests of Peru to the majestic cities of Prague and Amsterdam. Jenna's writing has appeared in The Boston Globe Magazine and The Morgan Horse.

Dear Girl,

I would like to impart to you some knowledge about the subject of the male species and how it may relate to your life. I realize that there are many more important things in your life, but this is a common source of great anguish and confusion and I will have accomplished a great deed if I can spare one person from this.

Once I reached a certain age, around twelve, I began to believe something – that I was supposed to be attracting boys. It was not something internal or that I particularly felt like doing, but everything around me was telling me otherwise. Magazines showed pretty, flirty dresses for "back to school," characters in television shows were obsessed with falling in love, and even family members were asking whether I had a boyfriend. The pressure is even worse today, with teenage pop stars dressing and acting as though they were sex professionals, yet attracting younger and younger girls who follow them, often holding them to idol-like status.

When this male attention finally fell upon me, I felt as though I had succeeded. I was finally pretty enough, thin enough, stylish enough, and had enough of whatever else it took to attract a boy. I was grateful for anything they gave or wanted from me. Other girls were very jealous and often cruel, but I held my head high, knowing that I had accomplished my duty of attracting a boy.

At the ripe old age of twenty-five, I have almost purged myself of this untruth, but not without great losses. I have fewer close girlfriends, and I still secretly crave to be noticed in a crowded room.

Dear girl, I want you to know that what beauty you possess is your own. Hold on to it, believe in it, nurture it and do not let anyone take it from you. No one can tell you when you are beautiful or worthy. Know it for yourself. If you are happy then you will possess and exude beauty. This is your strength; let it shine as much as possible. It will make others feel wonderful when its rays fall upon them. People should be grateful for the chance to become intimate with you, and if they are not, then you should not share your gift with them.

A true friend,
Jenna

Ava

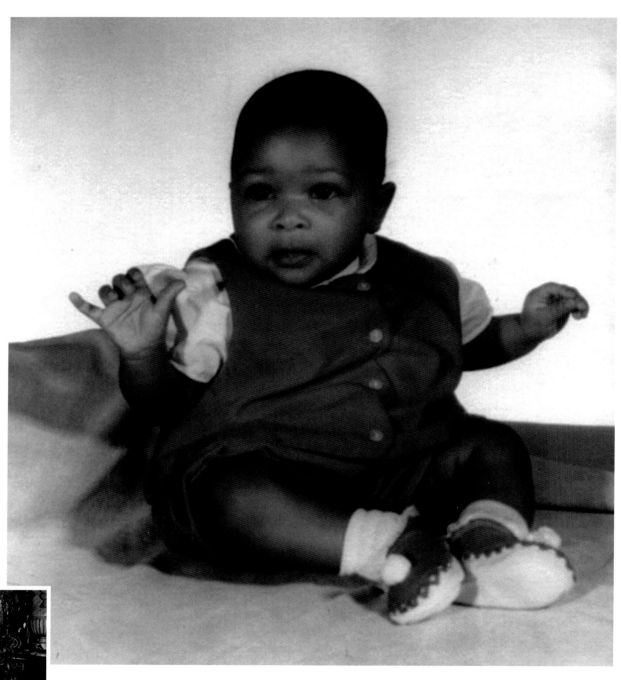

Ava Scott was born and raised in Winston-Salem, North Carolina. She grew up watching her dad make their family's famous Barbecue Sauce and playing the piano since before the age of 1. At The Madeira School is when she was first immersed in the beauty of "girl power" and the deep bonds between friends. She graduated from Emory University and has lived in Nashville for the last 15 years. She enjoys modeling, acting, reading suspense novels and her profession in Info Technology. She loves to spend money on friends, books, jewelry and clothes. Whatever is leftover is used to buy food!

Dear Sweetie Pie,

I hope that you find in your life the true meaning of friendship and how important it is to have friends and to be a friend. You don't need a lot of friends, but you do need true friends. It will be a life-long process to determine who they are.

Find people who you trust and who understand you — someone who will be there when you're happy and when you're sad. Laugh with them and celebrate life. Cry with them and celebrate life.

Accept that you will have different kinds of friends at different times. It's as if they somehow come along just as you need them. Some of the best memories are of times spent with extraordinary people who have touched my life and I am honored to call them friends. One of my best, best friends is amazing. She is radiant and full of life, just like the flower she's named after. I'll tell you some of the reasons why we are such great friends.

She loves pickles, but she's picky about them. I laugh until my eyes water because if the pickle has funny edges when it's cut, she won't eat it. I eat the pickles with funny edges.

She's the kind of friend who, if she wants to go out but you're not feeling very cute that day (maybe a pimple in the middle of your forehead or allergies that have your eyes swollen and puffy), it's OK. She understands and is willing to wait until you feel cute again.

She can mispronounce your mother's name and you don't get mad. You're not sure if your mom would think this was so funny.

She still comes over to your house even though your cat hisses and claws at her every time. You overlook it because this is the same cat who purred around the legs that boyfriend who you thought was great who wasn't so great.

She comes over to help take your drain apart when you drop one of your favorite earrings in the sink because she knows it would cost you an arm and a leg for a plumber.

You find that you switch personalities when you go on vacation together. You become the laid back, calm one and she becomes the bossy one.

You don't mind driving your car whenever you're going together because her driving scares you to death and she hates her car so much she would like to bury it one day.

This is the kind of friend who complements your life and that's what truly makes it a wonderful life.

Love ya, mean it!
Ava

Jane

Jane Cosner is the founder of youknow,youknow, an apparel company devoted to helping women feel beautiful on the inside as well as look great on the outside. She believes every woman has the ability to tap their inner essence to achieve their dreams. With a great love for new experiences, Jane is a Mom, an esthetician, a neuro-linguistic therapist, and now a successful business owner.

Dear One,

I so enjoyed spending time with you recently. I love to play your delightful games and answer your wonderful questions. Thank you for trusting me enough to listen to my opinion.

How will you know when you are doing the right thing?

As you move through your life, you will have so many fantastic opportunities to discover the answer to this question. In each set of circumstances, no matter how difficult they may seem, I know you will find the answer you are seeking in the feelings that are within you.

When you feel good you are in complete harmony with what is right for you, and that is your truest guidance. You can always count on this as you navigate your journey, situation by situation, toward the outcomes you desire.

Many times you will find yourself standing on the threshold of what appear to be tough choices. There will always be people or circumstances that do not line up with how you think things should be and you may find yourself feeling confusion or fear or anger. Although this may be frustrating, I encourage you to pay attention to these feelings; this is your guidance lovingly reminding you to reach for what feels best for you regardless of external events.

Each time you experience those negative emotions take as much time as you need and appreciate how the contrast of any situation helps you to be clearer about what is important to you. Once you know what that is then gather all of your will power and deliberately turn 100% of your attention toward that goal. I promise you that once this becomes a habit in your life you will feel the freedom of knowing that you are the architect, the director, and the storyteller of your life.

My dearest, your life will be whatever you believe is possible. You will never get it wrong. Take pleasure in your present. Know you will always be standing on new plateaus and reaching for new desires. Allow others their individuality; recognize that we each get to choose our life course. Seek joy in all that you do and you will always be guided toward what is right for you

Mon petite chou, life is an awesome adventure, enjoy your ride!

With great love for you,
Janie

Katie

Katie Younes, pictured to the right of her good friend, is an elite athlete scholar who started her athletic career as the only girl on her Little League baseball team and the only girl on her Pop Warner football team. Now Katie is an All-Star and All-League athlete in softball and field hockey and has traveled to Spain as a sports ambassador. She lives to compete!

Dear Friend,

As your life goes on and you get older, you will face many tough situations and, subsequently, tough decisions. With these times come happy and exciting moments, however, it's mostly the tough moments that I want to help you deal with.

There are many ways to deal with tough situations and there are different levels of severity. With every situation, you need to think out all the good things and bad things that could come out of that situation. This will help you make your decision.

You should never do something that you will regret. You should make your decisions for yourself, not for anyone else. You should do what makes you happy and follow your own instincts. Don't let anyone try to persuade you or get in the way of what you believe. That may sound selfish, but it isn't. There comes a time in life when you need to make decisions for yourself.

Always follow your dreams and don't let anyone or anything get in the way of your dreams.

There will be times when you feel like you want to just give up because things may be difficult and not going the way you want them to. This is the time that tests how strong you are and how much you want to reach your dream.

This is when you reach deep down inside yourself, pull out everything that is left in you to rise above the difficulty you are facing and put yourself back on the right track. If you are capable of doing this and can do it successfully, then you know you can survive anything.

With dreams come hard work, dedication, determination, and a will to never give up. That may seem like a lot, but if the dream is important enough to you, you won't even think twice about making the difficult decisions in life.

Katie

Maria

Maria Younes left civil war-torn Lebanon during the 1970s. She made spinach pies to raise money for her children and grandchildren so that they could travel to America. Maria is a matchmaker. An expert on love, she has successfully found wives for her son and grandson as shown in the picture above. She is the matriarch of a proud and successful American-Lebanese family. Her granddaughter Katie is also featured in Letters to a Girl.

A Conversation About Love, Marriage and Family

When did you get married?

 When I was 15 years old I was married. My first child, Joseph was born when I was 16 years old. I lived with my husband for 11 years and had five children. He died of an illness and left me a widow at the age of 26.

How did you support your family?

 We had some money in the bank but it was not enough. I had to sew, I had to be a nurse to earn enough money to take care of my children. I gave them everything they needed.

Why didn't you remarry?

 I was very pretty and lots of men came to marry me. But I didn't marry because of my children. I was still carrying my youngest in my arms. How could I sleep with another man with a baby?"

How important was it to stay near your children?

 I came to America with them. I worked like a horse. I worked in the kitchen of my son's restaurant. I didn't speak any English. So I went to night school, and I learned English. My children were all grown and had children of their own. I raised my oldest daughter's five children. She was always sick with asthma, so I raised the children.

How did you find the strength to keep going?

 One day I ended up in the hospital. It was my heart. I was dying. I could feel that I was dying and I prayed and I said, "My God, don't leave my kids working hard for me. They don't deserve that." And I swear to you, in 2 minutes I was awake.

 How did I do it? Where did I get my strength? I prayed to God morning and afternoon. I said to him, "How much do I love my children? I want to give them everything. Please help me to give my children everything."

How do you know when a woman is right for one of your sons?

 I have always had dreams that were true, that somehow were signs of things to come. My youngest son was divorced several times and I wanted him to be happy. One night I dreamt of him sleeping with a woman surrounded by children. When I woke up I said, "My God, this woman loves children." I didn't see her face, but at that moment I knew she existed.

 So he and I went to Lebanon to find her. I can always tell what a woman is like by the way she talks and by the words that come out of her mouth. I watched her and listened to her. I knew she was perfect. They were married and now have two beautiful sons. They've been married for seven years.

 I matched my grandson with the perfect woman too. I went to Lebanon, I looked around the village. I watched the women and I found the perfect woman for him. I watched the way she acted and again, the way she spoke and the words she used. This is how you tell.

Natasha

Natasha Koval-Paden is a mother, teacher and world-class pianist. Raised in the Ukraine, Natasha arrived in the United States with a scholarship to the Eastman School of Music. She later studied at Julliard. Since then, her career has spanned several continents and included programs with a number of distinguished orchestral and chamber groups. Natasha has a long-standing tradition of providing concerts for social welfare causes. The photo above was taken by Natasha's father before her very first piano recital.

Dear One,

Sharing is part of life! So I will share with you my path. I love music. My instrument happened to be piano. I loved listening and playing. Every new piece was a discovery that enriched me and my listeners. Performing and sharing beautiful masterpieces is what I do.

I grew up playing piano as a little girl in what was then the Soviet Union. The war made me a refugee, but I still kept on practicing even without a piano! I had drawn a keyboard with charcoal on a piece of cardboard, so that I could imagine the music. When the war was over, I could return to real pianos, and when I was fourteen I received a music scholarship to come to America to the Eastman School of Music. This was made possible by my "rescuer," Mr. Bill Sudduth (the grandfather of Jennifer Karin Sidford, editor of this book!), who worked for the United Nations Refugee Committee to help European refugee children and families with their resettlement. When I came to Rochester, New York, to prepare for school, I stayed at the YWCA. In my new country, I was fortunate to be able to perform concerts to call attention to the needs of refugee students. Nowadays I play only benefit concerts. My last concert was to raise support for college scholarships for women.
The next benefit will be for helping disadvantaged children and teenagers in Vermont, where I live. I also teach piano, and enjoy passing on the spirit of music.

Now what about you? You are unique on this earth. You alone can express what is inside you, inside your soul. Choose an art that really speaks to you! It may be singing, dancing, painting, or an instrument — it doesn't matter what. It will offer you a world of beauty. If you give yourself to this wonderful world of beauty, your needs will somehow be met, and one day you will be able to share your special gift.

My advice? Discover what is beautiful, cultivate it, and enjoy the joy of sharing.

Natasha

Pam

Pam Erickson recently helped to run one of the world's largest public relations firms from London and Cambridge, Massachusetts. She now works for E*TRADE Financial, bringing many years of her high tech experience to the dot com phenomenon. Graduating from Simmons College with a degree in journalism, Pam has been a reporter for The Patriot Ledger and The Boston Globe. She has also worked for the Democratic National Committee and many national- and state-level political campaigns. Pam is pictured here with her daughters Olivia and Audrey flying over London.

Dear Olivia and Audrey,

      As I watch a little girl, I am amazed and inspired. I am heartened by her strength, her sweetness, her courage, her tenacity, her imagination and her intelligence.   Her world seems to be a limitless supply of pure and magical moments. I am so fortunate to share in those moments — *her moments.*

      As I watch, I am proud. I am also sad, for the little girl grows up so fast and the magical moments of childhood pass so quickly. I wish I could change that.

      If I could, I would make each moment last much longer to be sure that the little girl might relish each one as it unfolds before her. I would tell her to hold on with all her might to the pride she feels when she masters the monkey bars, to the tenderness she shows an inch worm as she places it on a leaf, to the determination in her voice as she challenges her dad, to the certainty she expresses when she talks about the dog she will have someday, to the sheer glee she has as she lies in bed talking to her sister late into the night and to the confidence she radiates when she cracks the code on C - A - T.

      If these magical moments could be replayed over and over for years to come, they would forever guide the little girl as she evolves into the person she is meant to be. The little girl would always believe she could do anything. She would recognize that kindness and compassion create true success. She would cherish the beauty of her own spirit and know that others can never define her. She would remember that the word "can't" didn't exist when her world was new. She would rarely be intimidated and she would never take no for an answer. She would keep her mind open to new opportunities. She would strive to know herself and she would not be afraid to change. And, she would understand that the love of family and friends is more important than anything else.

      I hope always to know the little girl as she is today and I hope always to learn from her, for she has so much to teach.

With love,
Your Mom Pam

Jenny

Jennifer Karin Sidford is a mother of three very active boys and the creator of Letters to a Girl. She has written, ghostwritten and edited numerous articles and speeches for national and international companies during her 15-year career in public relations. Having traveled the globe for corporations such as Motorola, Hewlett-Packard, Apple and Dun & Bradstreet, she is happiest at home with her husband Chris and their sons, Ben, Jackson and Sam.

Photo: ©2003 Melissa Mermin

To all my nieces,

You are so lucky! There is no better place for a young girl to be than in America. Open your front door: Everything is in front of you and anything can be yours. In exchange for this great fortune, you need to be responsible for certain things. As women, here's our essential list:

Responsible for our Well-Being — We must take care of our health: our physical body and the lucidness of our minds. This must come first, before the needs of school, family, career and nation come calling. This will be one of your hardest tasks. If only One-a-Day vitamins helped us to remember the vital responsibility we have to ourselves to keep us healthy and happy. Only then, can we be responsible for anything, or anyone, else.

Responsible for our Bodies — The female body is the most celebrated form in the world. Keep it strong. Work out with weights, take Karate, walk five miles a day. Don't force your body to look like someone else's. Don't let anyone do anything to your body without your permission and your emotional consent. Whether it is someone you crave romantically or a doctor who believes you should have another medical test. You are in control and total control of what happens to you physically.

Responsible for Change — Before women worked side by side with men in boardrooms, courtrooms and operating rooms, we were a vital and thriving force of volunteerism. Society prevented us from building careers so instead we built a better society. We donated our skills and time to improve our country's greatest woes: discrimination, poverty, mental illness, disease. Noted anthropologist Margaret Mead said, "Never doubt that a small group of thoughtful, committed citizens can change the world. Indeed, it's the only thing that ever has." Women are particularly adept at this. We must continue volunteering as we continue to take charge in our paying jobs.

Responsible for Heart — We are the gender of love. The Ancient Greeks revered not one but five goddesses of love. As ambassadors of the heart, it is our responsibility to move humankind to a more loving existence. This can be done in very small ways, like sitting down with the unfairly labeled "freak" during school lunch, or in very large ways, like working hard to prevent a war between nations. Both are extremely significant actions of the heart.

With great faith in you,
Aunt Jenny

My Letter to You

My Letter to You

My Letter to You

Additional Acknowledgements

Many thanks to friends new and old that helped bring this book to fruition: Tom White for helping me to understand and successfully navigate the complicated world of self-publishing; Carrie Curley for creating a design worthy of the letters; Jennifer Sharkey for her enthusiastic offers to get whatever I needed; Cary Stratton Boyd for her impeccable proofing skills; Deborah Chiaravalloti for being ready with smelling salts and a good joke when the project seemed overwhelming; to all the early readers of the book's concept pages who took time to provide feedback; and, especially, to my husband Chris Sidford, for his "love always" and for understanding the charitable aspect of my project, and to my oldest son Ben, for his thoughtful input and for keeping me company during dozens of book errands in the summer of 2003.

100 percent of the editor's profits from the sale of this book are given to YWCA childcare, anti-violence, shelter, health, fitness and social justice programs for women and girls.

Please share this book with the women in your life and celebrate together the joy of growing up female.

If you would like to order additional copies, please call toll-free 800-838-3544 or order online at LetterstoaGirl.org.